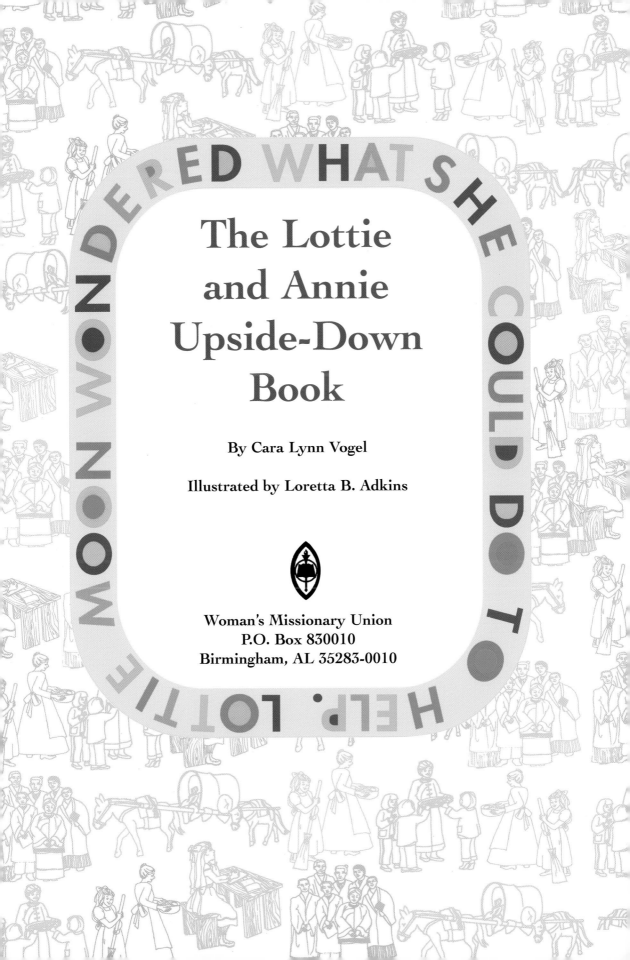

The Lottie and Annie Upside-Down Book

By Cara Lynn Vogel

Illustrated by Loretta B. Adkins

Woman's Missionary Union
P.O. Box 830010
Birmingham, AL 35283-0010

Lottie Moon lived a long time ago. When she was a little girl, she enjoyed running and climbing trees.

She liked to hear the stories that her mother would read to her brothers and sisters. Many times the stories were about missionaries.

As Lottie grew, she learned how to sew and cook and clean a house. She would watch her mother work very hard around the house.

Lottie Moon wondered what she could do to help.

CHINA

4

Lottie was very smart and liked school. She learned many languages in school.

When she grew up, she enjoyed teaching at a school for girls and in Sunday School in her town.

Lottie soon thought that God wanted her to be a missionary. She wanted to go and tell the people in China about Jesus.

Lottie Moon wondered what she could do to help.

Finally the day came when Lottie got news that she could go to China. She was so excited! She was going to China to be a missionary. She would live with her sister Eddie.

She traveled on a big ship. It took many days to cross the ocean. When Lottie arrived in China, she got off the big boat and climbed on a cart called a shentze [SHENT-zah]. It had two long poles fastened to two mules. One mule was in the front of the cart, and the other in the back. She went to a city called Tengchow [tongue-joe].

WONDERED WHAT SHE COULD DO TO HELP. LOTTIE MOON

In the city, the Chinese children liked Lottie. Lottie was not much taller than they were, and the children were very curious about her. They asked her many questions.

"What is your name?" "How old are you?" "Where do you live?"

Lottie liked the children, but they were speaking in Chinese. Lottie couldn't understand what they were saying.

Lottie Moon wondered what she could do to help.

must learn Chinese so I can talk to the children and women that I meet," Lottie told her sister.

I have an idea," said Lottie's sister. "You can come help me teach the boys in school how to read and write. That way you can learn more about the Chinese language."

Lottie was happy to help her sister at the school for boys. She worked hard to learn Chinese.

As Lottie and Eddie worked with the boys in the school, they began to think that girls needed a school, too. But Lottie and Eddie knew the Chinese people did not think that girls needed to go to school.

Lottie Moon wondered what she could do to help.

Later Lottie moved to a small village in China called Pingtu [ping-doo]. Lottie's house was very small with a dirt floor. The roof was made from straw.

Lottie invited people into her house. She baked cookies for them. The children especially loved eating her delicious cookies. While they visited with Lottie and ate the cookies, Lottie told them Bible stories.

While Lottie told the Bible stories to the children, some of the Chinese men would stand outside the open windows of her house. They listened to the stories, too. They liked hearing that Jesus loved them.

Lottie knew that more missionaries needed to come to China. Many people there needed to hear about Jesus.

Lottie Moon wondered what she could do to help.

11

So what did Lottie do to help her mother?

Lottie helped take care of her younger brothers and sisters when her mother had a lot of work to do. She also helped do chores around the house.

So what did Lottie do to help her sister?

Lottie helped her sister as she worked at the boys' school. While Lottie was helping at the school, she learned to speak Chinese.

So what did Lottie do to help the Chinese people?

Lottie invited the Chinese people into her home. She told them about Jesus. She also baked cookies for them.

So what did Lottie do to help get more missionaries to come to China?

Lottie wrote letters to the women where she had lived in America. She told them how she needed more missionaries to come and help her tell the Chinese people about Jesus. The women listened to Lottie and liked her idea. They saved their money and soon they had enough money to send three more missionaries to China.

So what did Lottie do to start a girls' school in China?

Lottie wrote more letters to the women back home. She told them that the girls in China needed a school. The women continued to save their money and soon they had money so Lottie could start the new school for girls. Lottie was thrilled!

Lottie Moon was a helper. She loved Jesus very much. She also loved the Chinese people. She made sure that the Chinese people knew that Jesus loved them, too!

Today, people can help missionaries all over the world by giving money to the Lottie Moon Christmas Offering® for International Missions.

Ideas for Parents, Teachers, and Caregivers

You and your preschooler may experience some of Lottie Moon's life by making this adapted recipe of her cookies. As you make the cookies, allow your preschooler to determine to whom you will give your cookies. Remind her that Lottie gave her cookies to the children in China to help them feel at home in her house.

Lottie's Cookie Recipe

1½ cup sugar
½ cup sour milk*
1 egg plus 1 egg white, well beaten
½ cup butter
4 cups flour
½ teaspoon soda

*(substitute 2 teaspoons vinegar plus enough milk to make ½ cup)

Preheat oven to 400°F. Cream butter and sugar; beat in milk and eggs. Stir in flour gradually to make a gooey dough. Turn onto floured surface. Coat hands with flour and pat dough thin (½ inch). Cut cookies into circles or other shapes. Bake for 8–10 minutes or until lightly browned. Makes a crisp, not-too-sweet cookie.

From *I Can Do That! 100+ Ways to Be On Mission* (Birmingham, AL: Woman's Missionary Union, 1999), 77.

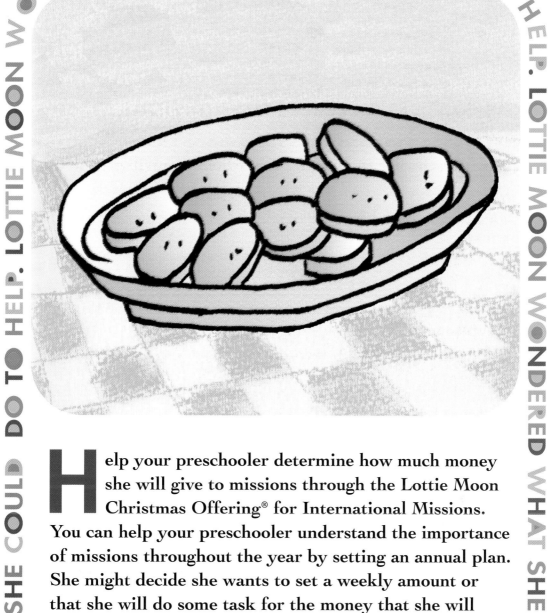

Help your preschooler determine how much money she will give to missions through the Lottie Moon Christmas Offering® for International Missions. You can help your preschooler understand the importance of missions throughout the year by setting an annual plan. She might decide she wants to set a weekly amount or that she will do some task for the money that she will give. Help to remind her of her commitment throughout the year. If you choose to set a goal for yourself, you can invite your preschooler to help you remain accountable as well. Make sure you celebrate your success throughout the year and when you make your gifts to the offering.

ANNIE ARMSTRONG WONDERED WHAT SHE COULD DO TO HELP.

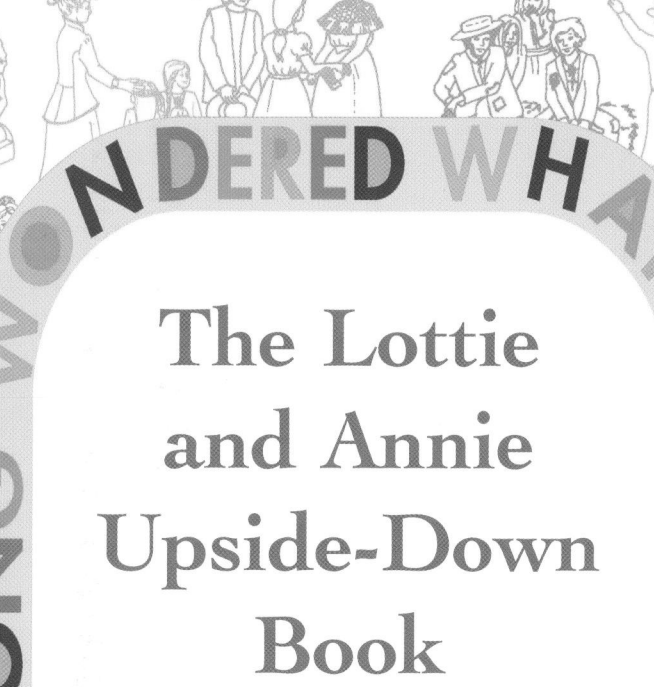

The Lottie
and Annie
Upside-Down
Book

By Cara Lynn Vogel

Illustrated by Loretta B. Adkins

Woman's Missionary Union
P.O. Box 830010
Birmingham, AL 35283-0010

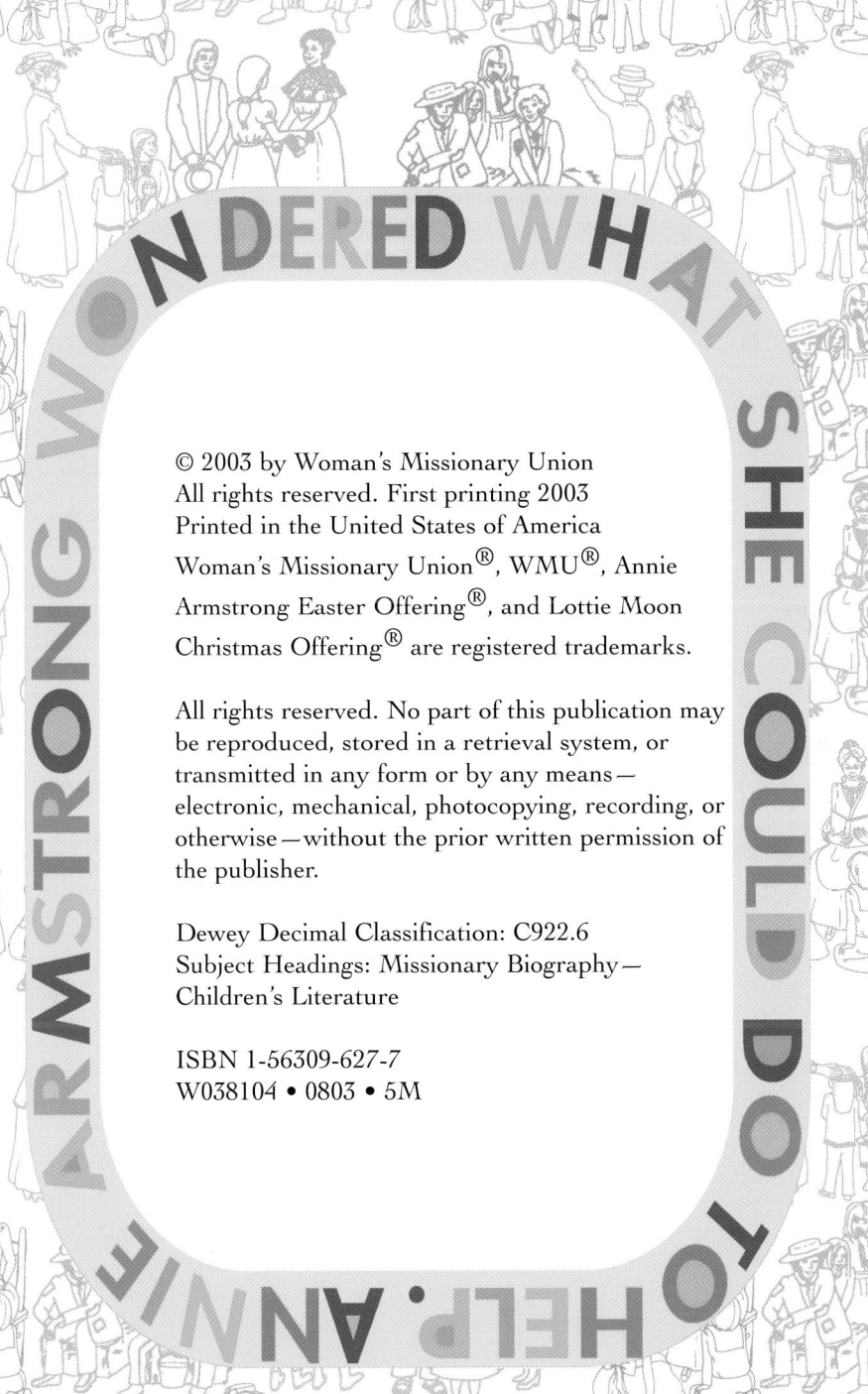

Dewey Decimal Classification: C922.6
Subject Headings: Missionary Biography—
Children's Literature

ISBN 1-56309-627-7
W038104 • 0803 • 5M

This book was lovingly created in the memory of my mother, Ann, and honor of my father, Jesse, who taught me about missions and developed my love of missionaries from my earliest memory.

Annie Armstrong lived a long time ago in a city with a big river. When she was a girl, she enjoyed going to look at the big ships with her brother James. It was fun to watch the ships come and go.

Annie and James saw many people from other countries at the port. When Annie grew up, she learned that many of these people could not speak or read English. Annie could tell that they were very lonely and scared in a new country.

Annie Armstrong wondered what she could do to help.

TO HELP. ANNIE ARMSTRONG WONDERED WHAT SHE COULD DO TO HELP. ANNIE ARMSTRONG WONDERED WHAT SHE COULD DO TO HELP. ANNIE ARMSTRONG WONDERED WHAT SHE COULD DO TO HELP. ANNIE ARMSTRONG WONDERED WHAT SHE COULD DO TO

Annie taught the children in her church. She helped them learn about the Bible. They liked hearing Miss Annie read them Bible stories.

Some of the children did not know about missionaries. They did not know that missionaries tell others about Jesus.

Annie wanted to help the children in her church know about missions and missionaries.

Annie Armstrong wondered what she could do to help.

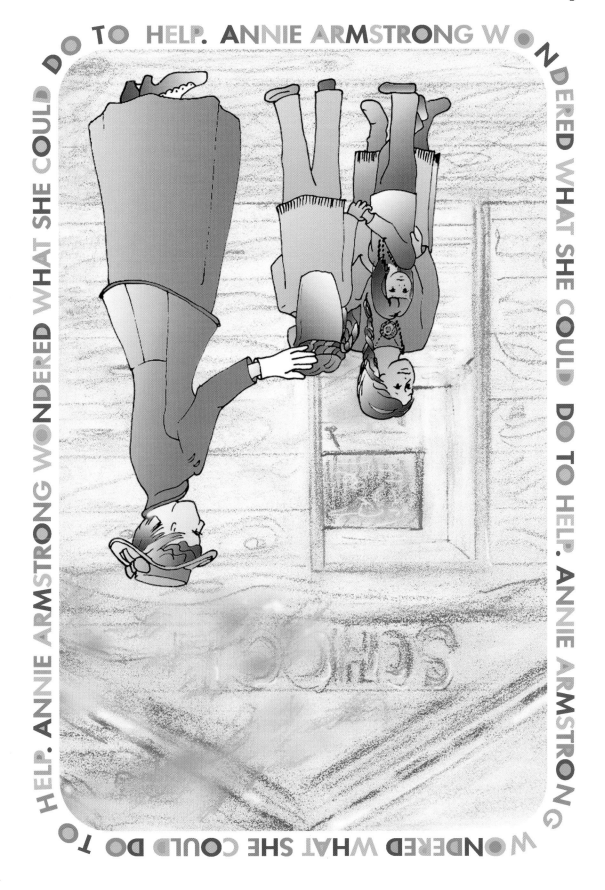

TO HELP. ANNIE ARMSTRONG WONDERED WHAT SHE COULD DO TO HELP. ANNIE ARMSTRONG WONDERED WHAT SHE COULD DO TO HELP. ANNIE ARMSTRONG WONDERED WHAT SHE COULD DO TO HELP. ANNIE ARMSTRONG WONDERED WHAT SHE COULD DO

Annie knew about some Native American (Indian) children who did not have new clothes for school. Annie knew these children needed clothes and people to care for them, too.

Annie remembered that missionaries were helping the Native American children. She knew that the missionaries did not have enough money for all the clothes they would need to buy for the children.

Annie Armstrong wondered what she could do to help.

DO TO HELP. ANNIE ARMSTRONG WONDERED WHAT SHE COULD DO TO HELP. ANNIE ARMSTRONG WONDERED WHAT SHE COULD DO TO HELP. ANNIE ARMSTRONG WONDERED WHAT SHE COULD DO TO HELP. ANNIE ARMSTRONG WONDERED WHAT SHE COULD DO TO

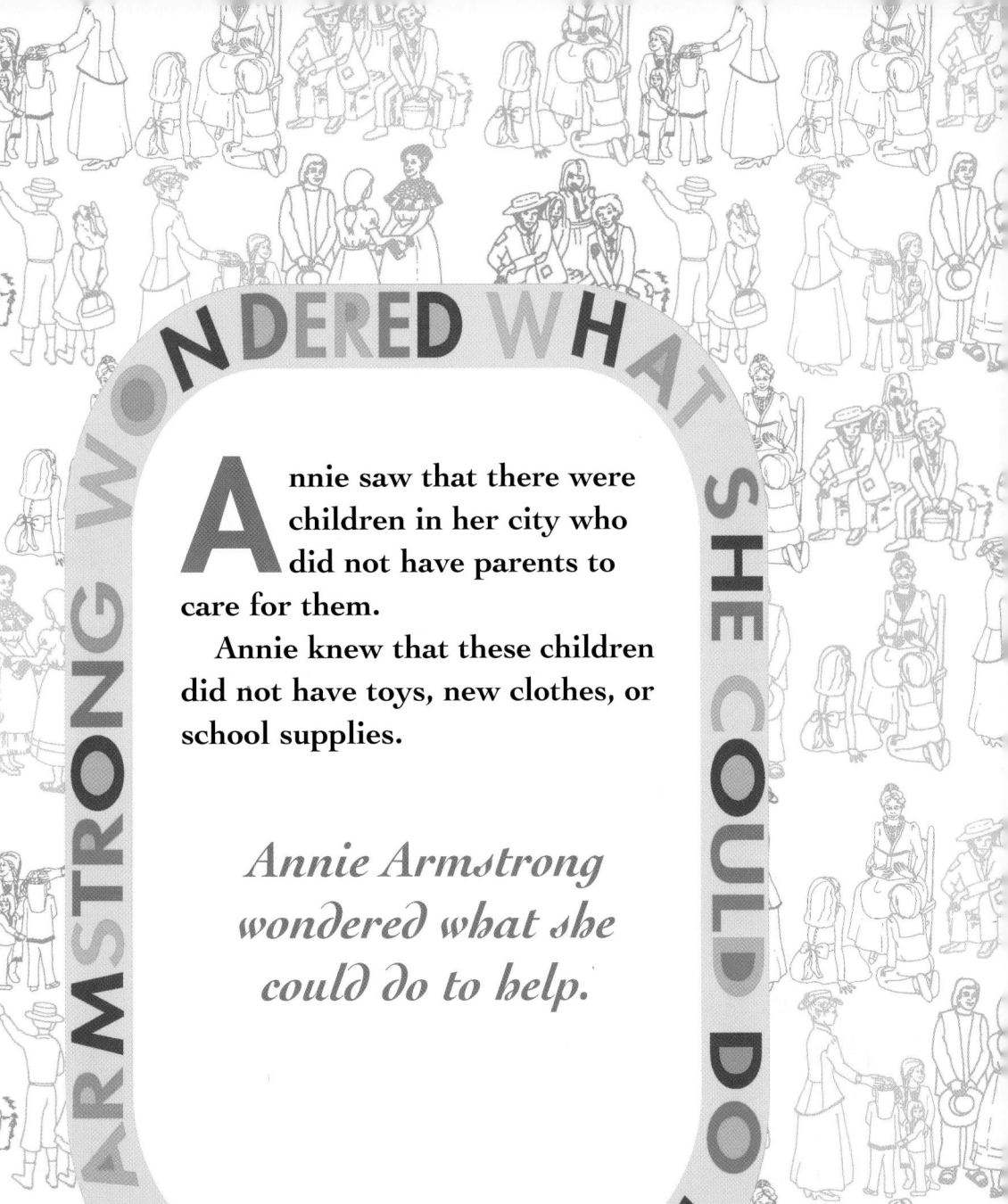

WONDERED WHAT SHE COULD DO TO HELP. ANNIE ARMSTRONG

Annie saw that there were children in her city who did not have parents to care for them.

Annie knew that these children did not have toys, new clothes, or school supplies.

Annie Armstrong wondered what she could do to help.

TO HELP. ANNIE ARMSTRONG WONDERED WHAT SHE COULD DO TO HELP. ANNIE ARMSTRONG WONDERED WHAT SHE COULD DO TO HELP. ANNIE ARMSTRONG WONDERED WHAT SHE COULD DO TO HELP. ANNIE ARMSTRONG WONDERED WHAT SHE COULD DO TO

Annie heard that people in Cuba needed a church building. Annie knew that these people did not have enough money to build a building.

Annie wondered if women in the United States could help the people in Cuba to have a church building.

Annie Armstrong wondered what she could do to help.

So what did Annie do to help the people from other countries she saw at the port?

Annie helped by getting a missionary to come and teach them to speak English. Soon they were making new friends.

So what did Annie do to help her Sunday School class learn about missionaries?

Annie taught them about missionaries and their work and how they helped people know about Jesus.

So what did Annie do to help the Native American children?

Annie asked some of the women in her church and other churches to sew clothes for the Native American children. The children were so happy to have new clothes for school!

So what did Annie do to help the children without parents?

Annie had a Christmas party for the children in her church. She asked them to bring money for the children without parents. With the money the children brought to the Christmas party, Annie was able to give Christmas gifts to the other children.

So what did Annie do to help the people in Cuba?

Annie helped to get money for the church in Cuba by asking people to give dimes. Those dimes added up to be enough money to build the new church building.

14

Annie Armstrong saw people who needed help and needed to know about Jesus. Annie decided to do something about it. Annie was a helper.

Today people give money to the Annie Armstrong Easter Offering® for North American Missions to help missionaries in North America tell more people about Jesus.

ANNIE ARMSTRONG
EASTER OFFERING
FOR NORTH AMERICAN MISSIONS

WONDERED WHAT SHE COULD DO TO HELP. ANNIE ARMSTRONG

Ideas for Parents, Teachers, and Caregivers

To encourage people to give to the Cuban church fund, Annie promoted the use of brick cards. Inside the card was a drawing of a brick wall with 20 bricks. Each brick was worth a dime. When a donation was made, the name of the donor was listed on the brick. When filled, the card was worth two dollars.

You and your preschoolers could design a "brick card" to help meet a need in the area of North American missions. Help your preschooler determine how to gather donations and help her understand how the money will be used.

Annie Armstrong also encouraged women to make "mite boxes" (named for the Bible story where the widow gave her two mites). Annie encouraged the women to place two pennies in the box each week for missions.

Your family may want to design a "mite box." Find a container or box, decorate it, and place it on a table or other often used space in your home. As money is placed in the "mite box," encourage your preschooler to give cheerfully.

Turn the book upside-down and go back to the other cover before continuing to read this book.

THE LOTTIE AND ANNIE UPSIDE DOWN BOOK

Turn the book upside-down and go back to the other cover before continuing to read this book.

THE LOTTIE AND ANNIE UPSIDE DOWN BOOK